A HEAD S.
Study Tips for the Student of

WESTERN CIVILIZATION:
A BRIEF HISTORY

VOLUME II: Since 1300

Jackson J. Spielvogel
The Pennsylvania State University

Prepared by
James T. Baker
Western Kentucky University

West/Wadsworth
I⊤P® An International Thomson Publishing Company

Belmont, CA • Albany, NY • Boston • Cincinnati • Johannesburg • London • Madrid • Melbourne
Mexico City • New York • Pacific Grove, CA • Scottsdale, AZ • Singapore • Tokyo • Toronto

COPYRIGHT © 1999 by Wadsworth Publishing Company
A Division of International Thomson Publishing Inc.
I(T)P® The ITP logo is a registered trademark under license.

Printed in Canada.
   3 4 5 6 7 8 9 10

For more information, contact Wadsworth Publishing Company, 10 Davis Drive, Belmont, CA 94002, or electronically at http://www.wadsworth.com.

International Thomson Publishing Europe
Berkshire House
168-173 High Holborn
London, WC1V 7AA, United Kingdom

International Thomson Editores
Seneca, 53
Colonia Polanco
11560 México D.F. México

Nelson ITP, Australia
102 Dodds Street
South Melbourne
Victoria 3205 Australia

International Thomson Publishing Asia
60 Albert Street #15-01
Albert Complex
Singapore 189969

Nelson Canada
1120 Birchmount Road
Scarborough, Ontario
Canada M1K 5G4

International Thomson Publishing Southern Africa
Building 18, Constantia Square
138 Sixteenth Road, P.O. Box 2459
Halfway House, 1685 South Africa

International Thomson Publishing Japan
Hirakawa-cho Kyowa Building, 3F
2-2-1 Hirakawa-cho
Chiyoda-ku
Tokyo 102, Japan

Senior Developmental Editor: Sharon Adams Poore
Editorial Assistant: Melissa Gleason
Ancillary Coordinator: Rita Jaramillo
Print Buyer: Judy Inouye

ISBN 0-534-56080-6

CONTENTS

PREFACE

This small booklet was designed to accompany your text *Western Civilization: A Brief History* by Jackson J. Spielvogel. I hope that it will give you a head start, a critical edge, toward success in your course. In it you will find four types of aids to help you master each chapter:

1.   A brief Outline to provide you with the broad scope of the chapter.
2.   Key Terms to identify—the most important persons, places, events, ideas, and works of art, literature, and music of each period.
3.   Questions for Critical Thought—questions that ask you to interpret and relate factual materials: important in preparing for essay examinations.
4.   Questions on the Primary Source Documents—questions that ask you to apply the information provided in the boxes of each chapter to the age from which they come.

As you begin this course, you might keep in mind a few simple hints gathered from teachers and former students in this course on how to study:

1.   Read before attending each class the text material that will be covered. Your instructor will provide you with a syllabus making clear what pages you should read.
2.   Study for relatively short periods (30-45 minutes) several times a week rather than waiting for long free periods. Read your text slowly and carefully, making yourself notes in the margins, and do not skip around from place to place.
3.   Once a week rewrite the notes you have taken in class. Notes can grow "cold" if left as they were taken for too long a time; and only "warm notes," ones that make sense, can help you on examinations.
4.   First master the big picture in each section, using the Outlines provided in this booklet; and then master the smaller details, using the section with Key Terms.
5.   Ask yourself questions about the material, using both the Questions for Critical Thought and the Questions on the Documents.

Teachers and former students have also offered a few tips on how to perform well in class:

1.   Be on time. Not only does this make the right impression on your instructor, but it prevents you from missing vital information about future classes, assignments, and examinations which are often given at the beginning of classes.

2.   Sit near the front. Studies have shown that those students who make the effort to sit close to the instructor hear better, see better, and remain more alert than those who sit further back.

3.   Do not sit with close friends. Many people feel that friends provide support, both emotional and educational, but friends can also distract you. If you sit with friends, be sure they understand that they must not take your mind off the central purpose for being there: to see, hear, and learn the material.

4.   Be rested when you come to class, stay alert, and take good notes. What happens in class is at least half of the course; and you should get as much from class lectures as possible. Do not feel that you have to take down the instructor's words verbatim. So long as you get the basic meaning, you will be in good shape.

5.   Should you have any kind of learning disability, talk with your instructor at the beginning of the course. Most instructors are willing to provide whatever additional help you may need; and you should not wait or hesitate to take advantage of this help.

The scores you make on tests will likely be the largest factor in determining the grade you make in this course; and so it is important that you do well on examinations. Here too are a few hints:

1.   Study regularly between examinations, not just the night before each one. If you have prepared all along the way, you need not "pull an all-nighter" in order to be ready. In fact, the all-nighter can do more harm than good. Being rested is vital to good performance on tests.

2.   As soon as you are given your test, look it over quickly, get an idea of its scope, and judge how much time you will need to complete each part.

3.   You will often be asked to identify persons, places, and events. Determine quickly how much time you have to identify each item, then give the basic facts about it but also its significance to the period you are studying. This added interpretive statement will demonstrate your superiority to the person with only superficial knowledge of the material.

4.   If your test asks you to match items, whether persons, concepts, or definitions, complete the ones you know before returning to any you may not be sure you know. Matching the ones you know will give you confidence, and by the process of elimination you may identify some you did not at first see.

5.   The same is true if you have to use a list of terms to fill in blanks. First use the ones you know, and you may then see better how to use those that remain.

You will probably be asked on your examinations to write essays. Essays not only test your knowledge of the facts but your ability to interpret and apply them. The exercises called Questions for Critical Thought and Questions on the Documents should be of help to you in preparing for essay questions. In addition let me offer you several suggestions on how to write essays that will both teach you and help you make high marks:

1. Read the entire question, and be sure that you understand exactly what is being asked and that you consider all parts of it. Address yourself only to the question that is asked, but address yourself to every section of it.

2. Make an outline before you begin to write the essay. Jot down in as few words as possible the major points you want to make, the most important persons, places, and ideas you want to include. Then glance back at your outline as you write so that you will not stay too long on one point or omit another.

3. Try to make one major point in your essay, with all of the others subordinate to it. This is your thesis. State it at the beginning, refer back to it at various appropriate times, and restate it briefly at the end. This will keep you focused on a unifying theme.

4. Write for an imaginary reader (who will be your teacher or an assistant, but you may not know exactly who it will be) who is intelligent but does not necessarily know the information you are relating. This way you will not fail to provide all information necessary to explain yourself, but you will also not insult your reader.

5. Be careful to spell correctly and to use good grammar. A history course is not an English course, and graders may or may not "count off" for poor spelling and grammar; but all graders are impressed either positively or negatively by the quality of your mechanics. While you may not see a specific comment about such matters on your essay, you may be sure that they have affected your final grade.

6. Think of an essay in a positive light. It should and can be an exercise in which the facts you have learned take focus and shape and make more sense than ever before. If done correctly, an essay can be the truest learning experience you can have and the most certain measure of your achievement.

I hope that this booklet adds to your enjoyment of the study of *Western Civilization*, increases your understanding of the ages you study, and helps you achieve high marks. I want to thank Elizabeth Jensen for her skill, accuracy, and speed in preparing it.

James T. Baker
Western Kentucky University

THE LATE MIDDLE AGES: CRISIS AND DISINTEGRATION IN THE FOURTEENTH CENTURY

CHAPTER

12

Outline:

I.   A Time of Troubles: Black Death and Social Crisis
    A.   Famine and Population Decline
    B.   The Black Death
    C.   Economic Dislocation and Social Upheaval

II.   War and Political Instability
    A.   The Hundred Years' War
    B.   Political Instability
    C.   England and France
    D.   The German Monarchy
    E.   The States of Italy

III. The Decline of the Church
    A.   Boniface VIII against Philip IV
    B.   The Avignon Papacy (1305-1378)
    C.   The Great Schism (1378-1415)
    D.   The Rise of Conciliarism

IV.   Culture and Society in an Age of Diversity
    A.   Vernacular Literature
    B.   Art and the Black Death
    C.   Changes in Urban Life
    D.   Inventions of Note

Key Terms:

1. Flagellant   *FLAGE*-ELL-ANT

2. Pogrom   *POH*-GROM

3. Ciompi   *CHOM*-PEE

4. Agincourt   *AGE*-IN-CORE

5. *Unam Sanctam*   *OON*-AHM *SANK*-TAHM

6. Avignon   AH-VEEN-*YON*

7. Conciliarism   KON-*SILL*-EE-ARE-ISIM

8. Giotto   JAH-TOE

Questions for Critical Thought:

1. Why were there peasant revolts in the fourteenth century? What forms did they take in various countries? What did they achieve?

2. What caused the Church's Great Schism, and what effects did it have on late medieval religious life? How did the average Christian carry on his/her religious devotions during the period when the Church was in such a state of chaos?

3. Why did late medieval writers begin to use vernacular languages? What resulted from this decision?

4. How did the plague called the Black Death affect the late medieval medical profession?

Questions on the Documents:

1. Describe the effects of the Black Death on individuals and cities. Why was it often attributed to the wrath of God?

2. Explain how superstition, fear, prejudice, and greed combined to cause the attack upon European Jews in 1349.

3.   Explain what would give a peasant girl like Joan of Arc the courage to follow the orders of her "voices" to death? What does this tell you about the medieval personality and its belief system?

4.   Discuss the claims Pope Boniface VIII made for papal authority in *Unam Sanctam*. What does the fact that this declaration caused such violent reaction say about prior understandings of papal power?

5.   In his *Comedy*, Dante used his ironic sense of humor to show how each sinner's punishment matched his sin. Use the case of Alessio Da Lucca to illustrate this point.

13 RECOVERY AND REBIRTH: THE AGE OF THE RENAISSANCE

Outline:

I.   Meaning and Characteristics of the Italian Renaissance
    A.   An Urban Society
    B.   An Age of Recovery
    C.   A Rebirth of Classical Culture
    D.   Recovery of the Individual

II. The Making of Renaissance Society
    A.   Economic Recovery
    B.   Social Changes

III. The Italian States in the Renaissance
    A.   The Five Major States: Milan, Venice, Florence, the Papal States, and Naples
    B.   The Examples of Federigo da Montefeltro and Isabella d'Este
    C.   Machiavelli and the New Statecraft

IV. The Intellectual Renaissance in Italy
    A.   Humanism
    B.   Humanism and Philosophy
    C.   Education
    D.   The Impact of Printing

V.   The Artistic Renaissance
    A.   The Early Renaissance
    B.   The High Renaissance
    C.   The Northern Artistic Renaissance

VI.   The European State in the Renaissance
    A.   The "New Monarchies"
    B.   Central Europe: The Holy Roman Empire
    C.   The Struggle for Strong Monarchy in Eastern Europe
    D.   The Ottoman Turks and the End of the Byzantine Empire

VII.   The Church in the Renaissance
    A.   The Problems of Heresy and Reform
    B.   The Renaissance Papacy

Key Terms:

1.	Castiglione	KAH-STEE-*LYOH*-NEE
2.	Isabella d'Este	EES-UH-*BELL*-UH *DES*-TEE
3.	Machiavelli	MAK-EE-AH-*VELL*-EE
4.	Pico della Mirandola	*PEE*-KO *DELL*-AH MEER-*AND*-OH-LA
5.	Vittorino da Feltre	VEE-TOR-*EE*-NOH DAH *FELL*-TREE
6.	Masaccio	MU-*SAH*-CHEE-OH
7.	Leonardo da Vinci	LEE-UH-*NAR*-DOH DAH *VIN*-CHEE
8.	Michelangelo	MIKE-EL-*AN*-GU-LOW

Questions for Critical Thought:

1.   In what sense can it be said that Machiavelli created a new political science? Describe it. What message does it have for modern readers?

2.   Define Renaissance humanism. Name the leading humanists, and tell what they wanted to and actually did accomplish.

3.   How did humanism affect Renaissance theories and practices of education? Give examples. Are they still pertinent?

4.   Compare and contrast the Northern and Southern forms of Renaissance art. Which is now considered more universal in appeal? Why?

5.   What kind of pope did the Renaissance produce? How did these popes affect the Renaissance?

Questions on the Documents:

1.   What conclusions can be drawn about the wealthy Renaissance man's diet and probable health by perusing the menu from one of Pope Pius V's banquets? Do you consider it unseemly for a pope and his guests to enjoy such food? Why or why not?

2.   According to the letters of Alessandra Strozzi, what characteristics and advantages did a Renaissance family look for when searching out a wife for one of its sons? What kind of marriage would he likely have?

3.   What was Machiavelli's advice to a prince who wanted to hold power? Do you feel that he is serious or in any way being sarcastic?

4.   What was the Renaissance image of man? Use Pico della Mirandola's *Oration* to demonstrate what the humanists believed man's nature and potential to be.

THE AGE OF REFORMATION

Outline:

I.   Prelude to Reformation
    A.   Christian (Northern Renaissance) Humanism
    B.   Erasmus and *The Praise of Folly*
    C.   Church and Religion on the Eve of the Reformation
    D.   Abuses of the Clergy
    E.   Popular Religion

II. Martin Luther and the Reformation in Germany
    A.   The Early Luther
    B.   The Development of Lutheranism
    C.   Germany and the Reformation: Religion and Politics
        1.   Emperor Charles V's Attempt to Preserve Christian Unity
        2.   The Peace of Augsburg: The Success of Lutheranism

III. The Spread of the Protestant Reformation
    A.   Ulrich Zwingli in Switzerland
    B.   The Radical Reformation: The Anabaptists
    C.   The Reformation in England
    D.   Calvinism

IV. The Social Impact of the Reformation
    A.   The Effect on Families
    B.   Religious Practices and Popular Culture

V.   The Catholic Reformation
    A.   Loyola and the Jesuits
    B.   A Revived Papacy
    C.   The Council of Trent

Key Terms:

1.   Thomas á Kempis   *TAHM*-US UH *KEMP*-US

2.   Indulgence   INN-*DULL*-GENZ

3.   Tetzel   *TET*-SELL

4.   Augsburg   *AHGS*-BURG

5.   Anabaptist   ANN-UH-*BAP*-TIST

6.   Predestination   PREE-DESS-TIN-*AY*-SHUN

7.   Jesuit   *JEZZ*-YOU-IT

8.   Matteo Ricci   MAH-*TAY*-OH *REECH*-EE

Questions for Critical Thought:

1.   Discuss the life and work of Desiderius Erasmus, showing his place in the Northern Renaissance and in preparing for the Reformation.

2.   Identify Martin Luther's part in the coming of the Protestant revolt. What personal qualities made Luther act as he did, and how did his actions affect the course of the Reformation?

3.   Discuss the Reformation in England. What caused it? How did it differ from the Reformation in other places? What were its results?

4.   Who was John Calvin, and what was Calvinism? Explain why and how he came to have such widespread influence in Protestantism?

5.   What shape did the Catholic Reformation take? How did the reformed Catholic Church differ from Protestantism? How well did its reforms prepare it for future ages?

Questions on the Documents:

1.   Show how and why Martin Luther's classroom exercise, The Ninety-Five Theses, caused such a sensation and had such an impact on his society and times.

2. Using the Marburg Colloquy as your guide, draw as many conclusions as you can about Luther's personality, mind, and public manner.

3. If Catherine Zell is typical of the Anabaptist faith, what new themes did this movement bring to Christianity? To what extent were these themes the natural consequences of Luther's doctrinal innovations?

4. If one follows Loyola's formula for correct Christian thinking, what does the Christian believe? How does the Christian act? What does the Christian accomplish?

15 DISCOVERY AND CRISIS IN THE SIXTEENTH AND SEVENTEENTH CENTURIES

Outline:

I. An Age of Discovery and Expansion
    A. The Motives Behind Them
    B. The Portuguese Maritime Empire
    C. Voyages to the New World
    D. The Spanish Empire
    E. Administration of the Empire
    F. The Impact of Expansion

II. Politics and Wars of Religion in the Sixteenth Century
    A. The French Wars of Religion (1562-1598)
    B. Philip II and Militant Catholicism
    C. Elizabeth's England

III. Economic and Social Crises
    A. Economic Declines
    B. The Witchcraft Craze

IV. Seventeenth-Century Crises: War and Rebellions
    A. The Thirty Years' War (1618-1648)
    B. Rebellions

V. Culture in a Turbulent World
    A. Art: Mannerism and Baroque
    C. A Golden Age of Literature

Key Terms:

1.   Vasco da Gama   *VASS*-KOH   DU   *GAAM*-AH

2.   *Encomienda*   INN-KOH-MEE-*INN*-DAH

3.   Huguenot   *YOU*-GHEN-OH

4.   Armada   ARE-*MAH*-DAH

5.   Mannerism   *MAN*-UR-IZ-UM

6.   Baroque   BAR-*OHK*

7.   Bernini   *BURR*-NEE-NEE

8.   Cervantes   SIR-*VAHN*-TEZ

Questions for Critical Thought:

1.   Describe the empire which the Spanish established in the Americas: its government, its social and religious systems, its economy, its strengths and weaknesses.

2.   In recounting the French religious wars, what peculiarly "French" characteristics do you find in them? What events in French history had helped create these characteristics?

3.   Describe the Elizabethan religious settlement in England. Was the Church of England Protestant or Catholic? Why did it work so well?

4.   Explain the witch hunt craze of the seventeenth century. What conditions fueled it, and why did it at long last end?

5.   Compare the lives and achievements of Montaigne, Shakespeare, and Cervantes. What do these men's careers tell you about each one's country in the sixteenth and seventeenth centuries?

Questions on the Documents:

1.   What did Cortes think of the Aztec civilization he conquered? What does he indicate made him feel justified in destroying it? What does this say about his own Spanish civilization?

2.   From the witchcraft case you have read, what "rules" of law did the witch hunters of the seventeenth century follow? How would a modern defense attorney attack their case?

3.   Describe the treatment of peasants on the farm captured by foreign soldiers during the Thirty Years' War, as recounted in the novel *Simplicius Simplicissimus*. To what extent do you see exaggeration for effect, and to what extent does this account agree with what you have read of treatment of civilians in other wars?

4.   How much of Shakespeare's tribute to England in "Richard II" is patriotism, how much xenophobia, and how much the dramatist's wish to please his audience? Give examples of your opinion.

RESPONSE TO CRISIS: STATE BUILDING AND THE SEARCH FOR ORDER IN THE SEVENTEENTH CENTURY

Outline:

I.   The Practice of Absolutism: Western Europe
      A.   France and Absolute Monarchy
      B.   The Decline of Spain

II.   Absolutism in Central, Eastern, and Northern Europe
      A.   The German States
      B.   From Muscovy to Russia

III. Limited Monarchy: The Dutch Republic and England

IV.   Economic Trends in the Seventeenth Century: Mercantilism and Colonies

V.   The World of Seventeenth-Century Culture
      A.   Art: French Classicism and Dutch Realism
      B.   The Theater: The Triumph of French Neoclassicism: Moliere

Key Terms:

1.   Absolutism   AB-SOH-*LUTE*-IZ-IM

2.   Richelieu   *RISH*-LOO

3.   Fronde   *FROHND*

4.   Colbert   KOLE-*BARE*

5.   Hohenzollerns   *HOE*-IN-ZOHL-URNS

6.   Habsburgs   *HABZ*-BERGZ

7.   *Leviathan*   LUH-*VYE*-UH-THUN

8.   Mercantilism   *MUR*-KAN-TEEL-IZ-UM

Questions for Critical Thought:

1.   List and explain the steps in Louis XIV's steady march toward absolute rule in France. What do you consider the most crucial steps for his eventual success?

2.   What factors transformed the rather unpromising German province of Brandenburg-Prussia into the core of what was to be a German nation? Explain each factor.

3.   Describe Peter Romanov's role in the emergence of modern Russia. Was he more or less important for Russia than Louis XIV was for France? Explain your answer.

4.   Describe the way a near-absolute monarchy became the world's first truly constitutional monarchy in Britain. What three persons do you feel contributed most to this change, and why?

5.   List and explain the new political theories that grew out of the Age of Absolutism. Show how each one was a product of its time.

Questions on the Documents:

1.   How do Louis XIV's *Memoirs* show that he had given some thought to the duties of a king? How well did his theory fit his actions?

2.   Explain how Peter Romanov's treatment of the rebellious Streltsy might demonstrate Machiavelli's notion that the effective ruler must act without consideration for the usual principles of morality.

3.   Explain how the 1688 British Bill of Rights paved the way for constitutional government. Show how this Bill influenced American colonists in the next century.

4.   How did Moliere satirize the world of scholarship? To what extent do you think his audience would have taken his joke seriously?

CHAPTER

Toward a New Heaven and a New Earth: The Scientific Revolution and the Emergence of Modern Science

17

Outline:

V.   Toward a New Earth: Descartes, Rationalism, and a New View of Humankind
    A.   Descartes' *Discourse on Method*
    B.   The Implications of Cartesian Dualism

VI.   Science and Religion in the Seventeenth Century
    A.   The Example of Galileo
    B.   Blaise Pascal and His *Pensées*

VII.   The Spread of Scientific Knowledge
    A.   Scientific Method: Bacon and Descartes
    B.   Scientific Societies
    C.   Science and Society

Key Terms:

1.   Hermetic   HUR-*MET*-IK

2.   Geocentric   GEE-OH-*SIN*-TRIK

3.   Heliocentric   HEEL-EE-OH-*SIN*-TRIK

4.   *Principia*   PRIN-*SIP*-EE-AH

5.   Vesalius   VUH-*SAIL*-EE-US

6.   Cartesian dualism   KAR-*TEEZ*-EE-UN *DEW*-AL-IZ-UM

7.   Spinoza   SPIN-*OH*-ZUH

8.   Pascal   PASS-*KAL*

Questions for Critical Thought:

1.   Discuss the causes of the Scientific Revolution of the seventeenth century. Of these causes, which seems the strangest to modern minds? Why?

2.   Discuss the men who added new knowledge to the field of medicine during the seventeenth century, and briefly describe each one's contribution to the field.

3.   Discuss the women who contributed to the Scientific Revolution, and briefly describe each one's contribution. Why did male scientists have such difficulties accepting them as equals?

4.   Describe the "scientific method," showing how you might use it to study a particular problem or question in a certain branch of science.

5.   How did the Scientific Revolution affect religious thought? How did religious thought affect the Revolution?

Questions on the Documents:

1.   Explain why Copernicus' heliocentric theory was at the same time so simple and so profound.

2.   What personality traits can you find in Galileo's account of his astronomical observations that would explain why he was a successful scientist?

3.   Speculate on why—amid the scientific progress of his century and despite evidence to the contrary—Spinoza was so unprepared to accept women as equals.

4.   What was at the root of Pascal's doubts about man's ability to find scientific certainty? What problems for future scientists did he accurately pose?

18 THE EIGHTEENTH CENTURY: AN AGE OF ENLIGHTENMENT

Outline:

I.   The Enlightenment
    A.   The Watchword: "Dare to Know"
    B.   Paths leading to the Enlightenment
    C.   The Philosophes and Their Ideas
    D.   Toward a "New Science of Man"
    E.   The Later Enlightenment
    F.   The "Women's Question" in the Enlightenment
    G.   The Social Environment of the Philosophes

II. Culture and Society in An Age of Enlightenment
    A.   Innovations in Art, Music, and Literature
    B.   The High Culture of the Eighteenth Century
    C.   Popular Culture

III. Religion and the Churches
    A.   Toleration and Religious Minorities
    B.   Popular Religion

Key Terms:

1.   Montesquieu   *MONT*-ESS-QUE

2.   Diderot   DEE-DUR-*OH*

3.   *Emile*   UH-*MEEL*

4.   Rococo   ROH-KOH-*KOH*

5.   Mozart   *MOHT*-ZAHRT

6.   Beccaria   BEK-*KAH-REE*-AH

7.   Carnival   KAR-NUH-*VAHL*

8.   Pietism   *PIE*-UH-TIZ-UM

Questions for Critical Thought:

1.   What was the "New Science of Man" that arose during the Enlightenment? What were its roots, and what did it add to man's self-awareness?

2.   Describe innovations in art, music, and literature during the Enlightenment. How did Enlightenment philosophy encourage and mold these innovations?

3.   What observations about women made by Mary Wollstonecraft in 1792 do you hear being repeated by feminists today, two centuries later?

4.   Through what media and in what forms did the ideas of the philosophes reach the better educated members of the general public?

5.   What happened to the various "state churches" of Europe under the attacks of Enlightenment critics? How did they respond to non-conformist minorities and new charismatic religious movements?

Questions on the Documents:

1.   Explain how and why Voltaire's attack on Christian intolerance proved effective. How might an orthodox Christian defend against such attacks?

2.   Briefly state the two arguments: a) that Rousseau's "general will" leads to democracy; b) that it leads to totalitarianism. What do you think?

3.   Show how Mary Wollstonecraft appealed both to men and to women in her call for the rights of woman. What kinds of people (men and women) would have responded favorably and what kinds would have responded unfavorably to her arguments?

4.   Describe the church services conducted by John Wesley and his Methodists. Explain why Wesley's Church of England did not welcome this movement.

19 THE EIGHTEENTH CENTURY: EUROPEAN STATES, INTERNATIONAL WARS, AND SOCIAL CHANGE

Outline:

I.   The European States
    A.   Enlightened Absolutism?
    B.   The Atlantic Seaboard States
    C.   Absolutism in Central and Eastern Europe
    D.   Enlightened Absolutism Revisited

II.   Wars and Diplomacy
    A.   The War of the Austrian Succession (1749-1748)
    B.   The Seven Years' War (1756-1763)
    C.   Armies and Warfare

III.   Economic Expansion and Social Change
    A.   Population and Food
    B.   New Methods of Finance and Industry
    C.   A Global Economy: Mercantile Empires and Worldwide Trade

IV.   The Social Order of the Eighteenth Century
    A.   The Peasants
    B.   The Nobility
    C.   The Inhabitants of Towns and Cities

Key Terms:

1.   Borough   *BURR*-OH

2.   Hanoverians   HANN-OH-*VAR*-EE-YUNS

3.	Junker	*YOON*-KUR
4.	Silesia	SIGH-*LEE*-SEE-YAH
5.	MariaTheresa	MAR-*EE*-AH TURR-*ACE*-UH
6.	Pugachev	*POO*-GUH-CHOFF
7.	Hierarchical	HIGH-UR-*ARK*-IK-UL
8.	Arkwright	ARK-RIHT

Questions for Critical Thought:

1. Define the term "Enlightened Despotism." Give three examples of enlightened despots of the eighteenth century, show why they were given the title, and indicate how enlightened each one actually was.

2. Describe the events and personalities that moved Britain during the eighteenth century from absolute to limited monarchy. Why did the same process not take place in France?

3. Describe daily life in the eighteenth century, particularly marriage, the family, and the treatment of children.

4. Discuss the progress made in eighteenth-century agriculture. What were the good and bad sides of such progress for peasants?

Questions on the Documents:

1. After reading the correspondence between Frederick of Prussia and his father, how would you think he probably described "the old man" to trusted friends his own age?

2. How would you know, even without being told, that the battle account from Quebec in 1759 was written by an Englishman? How would a French soldier have told it differently?

3. What do contemporary descriptions of slave trading tell you about white attitudes toward blacks? To what degree did they and did they not consider slaves humans?

4. Describe a debate that might have occurred between an advocate of free market economy and one who believes in government programs to help the poor in eighteenth-century France.

20 A Revolution in Politics: The Era of the French Revolution and Napoleon

Outline:

I.   The Beginnings of the Revolutionary Age: The American Revolution
   A.   Reorganization, Resistance, and Rebellion
   B.   The War for American Independence
   C.   Toward a New Nation

II.   The French Revolution
   A.   Its Background
   B.   The Destruction of the Old Regime
   C.   The Radical Revolution
   D.   A Nation in Arms
   E.   Committee of Public Safety, Robespierre, and the Reign of Terror
   F.   The "Republic of Virtue"
   G.   Reaction and the Directory

III. The Age of Napoleon
   A.   His Rise to Power
   B.   His Domestic Policies
   C.   His Grand Empire and the European Response

Key Terms:

1.   Saratoga   SAIR-UH-*TOH*-GAH

2.   Estates-General   ESS-*TAATZ JEN*-ER-UL

3.   Bastille   BAS-*TEE*-(L)

4.   Robespierre   ROBZ-PEE-*AIR*

5.   Thermidor   *THUR*-MUH-DOOR

6.   Coup d'etat   KOO DAY-*TAH*

7.   Code Napoléon   *KOHD* NU-POH-LEE-*OHN*

8.   Trafalgar   TRAH-*FAL*-GAR

Questions for Critical Thought:

1.   Describe the sequence of events that led to the American Declaration of Independence from Britain. Explain why you think the break was or was not inevitable.

2.   Outline the major events of the French Revolution from 1789 through 1804, and discuss four general principles of revolution to be found in this picture.

3.   What steps did the French revolutionaries take in 1783 through 1794 to ensure that there could be no return to the Old Regime? To what extent were they and were they not successful?

4.   List and discuss the major events that brought Napoleon Bonaparte to power in France. At what points might he have been stopped? How?

5.   Evaluate Napoleon as a military man and as a head of state. Did he fulfill or betray the revolution? Explain your conclusion.

Questions on the Documents:

1.   Pretend you are a moderate member of the British Parliament and have just read the American Declaration of Independence. What would you say in your next speech to that body?

2.   Describe the storming of the Bastille, and explain why this bloody event came to symbolize the French "triumph of justice and liberty."

3.   Use Anne Guinee's experience with the justice system during the reign of terror to show the insecurity of the regime that sought to make France a democracy.

4.   Pick out the words (nouns, adjectives, verbs) Napoleon used to create images and emotions that would inspire courage and determination among his men.

CHAPTER 21
THE INDUSTRIAL REVOLUTION AND ITS IMPACT ON EUROPEAN SOCIETY

Chapter *Outline:*

I. The Industrial Revolution in Great Britain
   - A. Its Origins and Causes
   - B. Technological Changes and New Forms of Industrial Organization
   - C. The Great Exhibition: Britain in 1851

II. The Spread of Industrialism
   - A. Industrialism on the Continent
   - B. The Industrial Revolution in the United States

III. The Social Impact of the Industrial Revolution
   - A. Growth in Population
   - B. Growth of Cities
   - C. A New Industrial Middle Class
   - D. A New Working Class
   - E. Working Conditions
   - F. Worker Efforts at Change
   - G. Government Efforts at Change

Key Terms:

1. Capital   *KAP*-IT-UL

2. Crystal Palace   *KRIS*-TUL *PAL*-US

3. Bourgeois   BOOR-*GWAH*

4. Proletariat   PRO-LUH-*TARE*-EE-UT

5.   Luddite   *LUDD*-EYET

6.   Chartism   *CHART*-IZ-UM

Questions for Critical Thought:

1.   Explain how and why the Great Exhibition of 1851 came to symbolize the Industrial Revolution and Britain's place in it.

2.   Show how and why the Continental Industrial Revolution differed from that of Britain. Why did it eventually surpass the productivity of its island competitor?

3.   Show how and why the Industrial Revolution in the United States differed from both the British and the Continental ones. What factors favored eventual American superiority?

4.   Discuss the social impact (the effect on daily life) of the Industrial Revolution. Show how we are still today living with its social consequences.

5.   Discuss the various reactions to industrial abuses. What remedies were offered, by whom were they offered, and how successful were they?

Questions on the Documents:

1.   List the traits Edward Baines said made Richard Arkwright a successful entrepreneur. Then list conditions, advantages, and probable personal traits that Baines failed to mention but which hindsight tells us also helped.

2.   Describe the likely appearance and personality of a man or woman who had worked for five years under the rules of the Berlin Trading Company.

3.   What commentary, hidden in his description of a steamship's arrival, was Mark Twain making about effects on American life of the Industrial Revolution? Is he for it or against it?

4.   What would you, a reform-minded member of the British Parliament, have recommended the government do about child labor abuse? What would you have recommended as punishment for sadistic overseers?

CHAPTER
22 REACTION, REVOLUTION, AND ROMANTICISM, 1815-1850

Outline:

I. The Conservative Order, 1815-1850
    A. Peace Settlement After Napoleon
    B. The Conservative Domination: The Concert of Europe
    C. Revolt in Latin America
    D. The Greek Revolt
    E. Conservative Domination

II. The Ideologies of Change
     A. Liberalism: John Stuart Mill
     B. Nationalism
     C. Early Socialism: Robert Owen

III. Revolution and Reform, 1830-1850
      A. The Revolutions of 1830
      B. The Revolutions of 1848
      C. Growth of the United States

IV. Culture in An Age of Reaction and Revolution: The Mood of Romanticism
     A. Characteristics of Romanticism
     B. Romantic Poets and the Love of Nature
     C. Romanticism in Art and Music

Key Terms:

1. Metternich   *MET*-UR-NIK

2. Bourbon   BOOR-*BONE*

3. Tory   *TOH*-REE

4.	Louis-Philippe	LOO-EE-FILL-*EEP*
5.	Mazzini	MAT-*ZEEN*-EE
6.	Goethe	*GET*-TUH
7.	Delacroix	*DEL*-UH-KRAW
8.	Beethoven	*BAY*-TOH-VAN

Questions for Critical Thought:

1. Outline the agreement devised at the Congress of Vienna. How did it seek to establish a balance of power? Why is it called a Monument to Conservatism?

2. Explain the ideology of nineteenth-century Conservatism, and show how it both dominated and provoked reaction during the period from 1815 to 1848.

3. Compare and contrast the period 1815-1870 in Britain and in France. Account for the different set of events and final results.

4. Define Romanticism. Discuss its characteristics, its major representatives, the various fields of the arts it affected, and what its lasting achievements were.

Questions on the Documents:

1. According to Austria's Prince Metternich, what characteristics of a nation give its people security and stability? Explain how each characteristic contributes to the whole.

2. How do John Stuart Mill's views on "liberty" reflect the death of an old world and the birth of a new one? How will such ideas be tested in the next century?

3. Describe the enthusiasm of young German liberals like Carl Schurz when their long-awaited revolution seemed at hand. Suggest three probable reactions among such young men when they realized it had failed.

4. Explain the nineteenth century's love for "Gothic" literature, particularly its tendency to combine romance and horror, as illustrated by the writings of Edgar Allen Poe. What does this say about the age—and the Romantic Movement?

CHAPTER 23

An Age of Nationalism and Realism, 1850-1871

Outline:

I. The France of Napoleon III
    A. Louis Napoleon and the Second Napoleonic Empire
    B. Foreign Policy: the Crimean War

II. National Unification: Italy and Germany

III. Nation Building and Reform
    A. The Austrian Empire: Toward a Dual Monarchy
    B. Imperial Russia
    C. Britain's Victorian Age
    D. The United States: Civil War and Reunion
    E. Canadian Nationhood

IV. Industrialization and the Marxist Response
    A. Prosperity and Trade
    B. Marx and Marxism

V. Science and Culture in An Age of Realism
    A. A New Age of Science
    B. Darwin and the Theory of Organic Evolution
    C. Realism in Literature and Art

Key Terms:

1. *Realpolitik*   REE-*AL*-POLE-IT-*EEK*

2. Cavour   KAH-*VOOR*

3.	Garibaldi	GARE-UH-*BALD*-EE
4.	Bismarck	*BIZZ*-MARK
5.	Disraeli	DIZZ-*RAY*-LEE
6.	Pasteur	PAST-*YOUR*
7.	Flaubert	FLOW-*BEAR*
8.	Courbet	KOOR-*BAY*

Questions for Critical Thought:

1. Describe the unification of Italy. Show how men and historical circumstances cooperated to achieve the dream of *risorgimento*.

2. Explain how Bismarck accomplished the unification of Germany. What kind of legacy did he leave his people and nation?

3. Explain the theories of Karl Marx. What circumstances, political and personal, led him to them? Why would they so strongly appeal to radical reformers?

4. Define the term "Realism" as applied to the literature and art of the late nineteenth century. Give examples of it, and show its legacy for our own day.

Questions on the Documents:

1. Explain how Bismarck "edited" his king's telegram from Ems to make the French feel they had been insulted. What was his purpose in doing this, and how well did he succeed?

2. Compare and contrast the emancipation proclamations of Tsar Alexander II and Abraham Lincoln. Which was the more thorough and why?

3. Having read Marx's description of the way we will arrive at the classless society, how would you judge Marx's opinion of man's nature?

4. What made Charles Dickens' description of industrial Birmingham so powerful? What does his portrayal say about his own feelings on the subject?

24 MASS SOCIETY IN AN "AGE OF PROGRESS," 1871-1894

Outline:

I. The Growth of Industrial Prosperity
- A. New Products and New Markets
- B. New Patterns in An Industrial Economy
- C. Women and New Job Opportunities
- D. Organizing the Working Class

II. The Emergence of Mass Society
- A. Population Growth
- B. Transformation of the Urban Environment
- C. The Social Structure of Mass Society
- D. The Role of Women
- E. The Middle-Class and Working-Class Family
- F. Education and Leisure in An Age of Mass Society

III. The National State
- A. Political Democracy in Western Europe
- B. Persistence of the Old Order in Central and Eastern Europe

Key Terms:

1. Zeppelin   *ZEP*-UH-LINN

2. Cartel   KAR-*TELL*

3. Liebknecht   *LEEB*-NECKED

4. Bernstein   *BURN*-STYNE

5.	Ruhr	*ROOR*
6.	Vanderbilt	*VAN*-DUR-BUILT
7.	Gladstone	*GLAD*-STONE
8.	*Kulturkampf*	*KUL*-TUR-KAHMF

Questions for Critical Thought:

1. Explain and describe the rise of socialism in its various forms after 1870. What caused its diffusion, and what were its attractions?

2. Describe the urbanization of Europe in the late nineteenth century, and how it both created problems and solved them.

3. What were the various roles of women in the new social structure? Did women live better or worse lives than in previous times?

4. Compare the democracies of Britain and France. How did each nation's history contribute to these developments?

5. How does Russia's history at the old century's end explain its violent history in the century to come?

Questions on the Documents:

1. Explain why department stores proved so successful. What needs did they satisfy, and what sound economic principles did they follow?

2. Using Octavia Hill as your example, show how early reformers combined compassion for the poor with shrewd business sense.

3. Give the response one of today's feminists might make to Elizabeth Poole Sanford's advice to women.

4. Describe the hysteria that led to the Paris Commune of 1871. What made you trust or distrust Clemenceau's account of the events in Montmartre?

25 AN AGE OF MODERNITY AND ANXIETY, 1894-1914

Outline:

I. Toward the Modern Consciousness: Intellectual and Cultural Developments
    A. The Emergence of a New Physics
    B. Sigmund Freud and Pyschoanalysis
    C. Social Darwinism and Racism
    D. Attack on Christianity and Church Responses
    E. The Culture of Modernity: Literature, Art, and Music

II. Politics: New Directions, New Uncertainties
    A. The Women's Rights Movement
    B. Jews and Nationalism
    C. Liberalism Transformed
    D. Growing Tensions in Germany
    E. Imperial Russia
    F. The Rise of the United States

III. The New Imperialism
    A. Causes
    B. The Creation of Empires: Africa and Asia

IV. International Rivalry and the Coming of War
    A. The Bismarckian System of Alliances
    B. New Directions and New Crises

Key Terms:

1.	Quanta	*KWAHNT*-UH
2.	*Volk*	*FOHLK*
3.	Stravinsky	STRAH-*VIN*-SKEE
4.	Zionism	*ZY*-OHN-IZ-UM
5.	Boer	*BORE*
6.	Rhodesia	ROH-*DEEZ*-EE-UH
7.	Manchus	MAN-*CHOOZ*
8.	Siam	SIGH-*AM*

Questions for Critical Thought:

1. How did Freud's analysis of human nature depart from previous analyses? To what extent did Freudian analysis become "the future" of anthropology?

2. Explain Social Darwinism, and show how it helped give direction and legitimacy to a new wave of racism. What were Jewish responses to the related phenomenon of anti-Semitism?

3. How and why did the feminist movement come about? In what ways was it a product of its times?

4. Describe the "New Imperialism" of the late nineteenth century. How was it different from the earlier imperialism? What were its causes and results?

5. How did Europe's Asian and African empires differ? Why? What were the reactions of already established nations in each continent to these empires?

Questions on the Documents:

1. What do you learn of Freud's methodology by reading his lecture on repression? What explanation do you find here for the immense prestige he gained in his own lifetime?

2.   How would a typical woman of 1879 have felt watching Ibsen's *A Doll's House*? What might "Nora" have said to such women had she turned to address the audience directly?

3.   What was Kipling's "white man's burden," how were white men to bear it, and what would be their reward?

4.   In his 1908 interview with the British *Daily Telegraph*, Kaiser William II spoke his mind. What did he mean to say, and how did he end up saying it? How do you account for the difference?

THE BEGINNING OF THE TWENTIETH-CENTURY CRISIS: WAR AND REVOLUTION

Outline:

I.   The Road to World War I
      A.   Nationalism and Internal Dissent
      B.   Militarism
      C.   Outbreak of War: The Summer of 1914

II.   The War
      A.   Illusions and Stalemate: 1914-1915
      B.   The Great Slaughter: 1916-1917
      C.   The Widening of the War
      D.   The Impact of Total War on the Home Front

III. War and Revolution
      A.   The Russian Revolution
      B.   The Last Year of the War: 1918

IV.   The Paris Peace Settlement
      A.   The Big Four
      B.   The Treaty of Versailles

Key Terms:

1.   Balkans   *BALL*-KINZ

2.   Gallipoli   GAL-*IP*-OH-LEE

3.   Lusitania   LOOS-UH-*TANE*-EE-UH

4.	Rasputin	RAS-*PEW*-TIN
5.	Hemophilia	HEEM-OH-*FEEL*-EE-UH
6.	Lenin	*LYN*-IN
7.	Bolshevik	*BOWL*-SHEE-VIK
8.	Reparations	REP-ARE-*A*-SHUNZ

Questions for Critical Thought:

1. What were the conditions, factors, and events that led—both directly and indirectly—to the outbreak of World War I?

2. What impact did a total war such as World War I have on life back home in the countries involved? How were domestic, economic, and political moments affected by it?

3. Recount the story of the Russian Revolution from the abdication of the Tsar until the end of the ensuing civil war. How do these events help explain Russia today?

4. Describe the Paris Peace Conference and the Treaty of Versailles. To what degree and in what ways were they and were they not successful?

Questions on the Documents:

1. Why would you know, had you not been told, that Remarque himself had known trench warfare? Explain how he made his account of it so powerful.

2. What does Naomi Loughnan indicate she learned in her munitions factory about working-class men and women? What were various classes and genders learning from each other there?

3. From John Reed's account, what do you think made Lenin the leader of the Russian Revolution? What does Reed mean by Lenin's "intellect"?

4. How did Woodrow Wilson and Georges Clemenceau differ in their assessments of the war? Why did Clemenceau consider Wilson naive and Wilson consider Clemenceau a vindictive bigot?

THE FUTILE SEARCH FOR A NEW STABILITY: EUROPE BETWEEN THE WARS, 1919-1939

Outline:

I.   An Uncertain Peace: The Search for Security
     A.   French Policy of Coercion
     B.   The Great Depression

II. The Democratic States
     A.   Great Britain
     B.   France
     C.   The United States and Roosevelt's New Deal

III. Retreat from Democracy: Authoritarian and Totalitarian States
     A.   Fascist Italy
     B.   Hitler and Nazi Germany
     C.   Soviet Russia
     D.   Authoritarian States

IV. The Expansion of Mass Culture and Mass Leisure
     A.   Radio and Film
     B.   Mass Leisure

V.   Cultural and Intellectual Trends in the Interwar Years
     A.   Nightmares and New Visions
     B.   Jungian Psychology
     C.   The Heroic Age of Physics

Key Terms:

1.   Briand   BREE-*AHN*

2.   Fascism   *FASH*-IZ-UM

3.   Lateran Accords   *LAT*-UR-INN AK-*KORDZ*

4.   Weimar   *VYE*-MAR

5.   *Mein Kampf*   MINE   *KAHMF*

6.   Aryianism   *AIR*-EE-AN-IZ-UM

7.   *Kristallnacht*   KRISS-*TAHL*-NAHKT

8.   Dali   *DOLL*-EE

Questions for Critical Thought:

1.   How did the Western democracies react and respond differently to the Great Depression? Explain why the reactions and responses were so varied.

2.   Describe and explain the European retreat from democracy and move toward totalitarianism in the time between the wars. Why did this happen where it happened, and what were the consequences?

3.   Discuss the Nazi movement and its rise to power. What part did Adolf Hitler play? What kind of state and society did Nazism build?

4.   What happened in the Soviet Union between the wars? How does the Stalinist era help explain contemporary events there?

5.   What forms did art, music, philosophy, and literature take between the wars? How are these forms reflections of the age?

Questions on the Documents:

1.   Describe the results of unemployment during the Great Depression. How would a fascist politician have appealed for the votes of unemployed men?

2.   What did Hitler think mass political meetings accomplished? How did he try in speeches to maximize the effects of these meetings?

3.   Explain how the Soviet collective farm worked and why there was continual resistance to it by peasants.

4.   What "state of mind" was Dadaism? Explain your answer as a Dada artist might have done.

CHAPTER 28

THE DEEPENING OF THE EUROPEAN CRISIS: WORLD WAR II

Outline:

I.   Prelude to War, 1933-1939
    A.   The "Diplomatic Revolution," 1933-1937
    B.   The Path to War, 1938-1939

II.   The Course of World War II
    A.   Victory and Stalemate
    B.   The War in Asia: Pearl Harbor
    C.   The Turning Point of the War, 1942-1943
    D.   The Last Years of the War, 1944-1945

III. The Nazi New Order
    A.   The Nazi Empire
    B.   The Holocaust

IV.   The Home Front
    A.   The Mobilization of Peoples
    B.   The Frontline Civilians: The Bombing of Cities

V.   The Aftermath of the War: The Emergence of the Cold War
    A.   The Conferences at Teheran, Yalta, and Potsdam
    B.   The "Iron Curtain"

Key Terms:

1.	Sudetenland	SOO-*DEBT*-INN-LAHND
2.	*Blitzkrieg*	*BLITS*-KREEK
3.	Vichy	*VISH*-EE
4.	*Luftwaffe*	*LOOFT*-VAFF-UH
5.	Stalingrad	*STAHL*-INN-GRAHD
6.	Holocaust	*HOL*-OH-KOST
7.	Auschwitz	*OWSH*-WITS
8.	Hiroshima	HEE-*ROH*-SHEE-MAH

Questions for Critical Thought:

1. Describe the "diplomatic revolution" that Hitler began after 1933. Explain how this revolution led eventually to war.

2. Tell the story of the first two years of World War II. If you had been reporting from the field in October 1942, what would you have predicted? Why?

3. Describe the Nazi Empire: its organization, what it sought to accomplish, and its relative success. How does the Holocaust fit into the overall picture?

4. Describe what it was like to live in a "front line" city during the war. To what extent did bombing affect the outcome of the war?

5. Reviewing the Big Three wartime conferences, show the origins of the Cold War. Where exactly were crucial mistakes made—and by whom?

Questions on the Documents:

1. Compare and contrast the two interpretations—by Churchill and Chamberlain—of the Munich agreement. At that point in history, which sounded more plausible? Explain.

2.   Using the German soldier's diary, recount how the German army in Russia lost heart. Why do you not find this man cursing Der Fuhrer?

3.   Recount the systematic way people at German extermination camps were dispatched. What reasoning stood behind such a system?

4.   How did aerial bombing change the nature and character of war? Describe its effects on people in cities under bombardment.

COLD WAR AND A NEW EUROPE, 1945-1970

Outline:

I.   The Development of the Cold War
     A.   Confrontation of the Superpowers
     B.   The Cuban Missile Crisis and Détente

II. Recovery and Renewal in Europe
     A.   The End of European Colonies
     B.   The Soviet Union: From Stalin to Khrushchev
     C.   Western Europe's Revival of Democracy and the Economy
     D.   Western Europe's Move Toward Unity

III. The Emergence of a New Society
     A.   The Structure of European Society
     B.   The Permissive Society
     C.   Education and Student Revolt

Key Terms:

1.   NATO   *NAY*-TOH

2.   Vietnam   VEE-ETT-*NAHM*

3.   Ho Chi Minh   HOH   CHEE   *MEN*

4.   Nikita Khrushchev   NUH-*KEE*-TUH   *KROO*-SHOF

5.   Alexander Solzhenitsyn   AL-EX-*AND*-UR   SOLZ-INN-*EAT*-SIN

6.   Alexander Dubcek   AL-EX-*AND*-UR *DOOB*-CHEK

7.   Charles De Gaulle   *SHARL* DAY-*GOLL*

8.   Ludwig Erhard   *LOOD*-VIK *AIR*-HEART

Questions for Critical Thought:

1.   What were the causes of the Cold War? What issues continued through the 1950s and 1960s to divide East and West? Did world leaders make things better or worse?

2.   How did "decolonization" affect both the First World and the Third World? What kind of world would we have today had "decolonization" been slower and more peaceful?

3.   Trace the history of the Soviet Bloc from 1945 to 1970. To what degree did its rivalry with the West create its policies and directions? How did it in turn affect those in the West?

4.   What areas of the citizen's life were affected by the experiments in the welfare state adopted by Western democracies after World War II? What are the benefits and problems of the welfare state?

5.   Discuss the causes and effects of the "permissive" society of post-war Europe. In what ways are we still living under its influence?

Questions on the Documents:

1.   Explain the Truman Doctrine. What threat provoked it, what was its intent, and where did it lead? What similar threats later appeared, and how did subsequent presidents respond to them?

2.   Compare Khrushchev's account of the Cuban Missile Crisis with what you know of the American version of this event. Who was really the aggressor, and who really won?

3.   How does the 1956 uprising against Soviet rule in Hungary look today, when Hungary is free of foreign domination? What now seems to be its significance? Will today's view continue?

4.   If Bob Dylan's song is truly an anthem for the protest movements of the 1960s, what groups did protestors want to hear their complaints and why?

THE CONTEMPORARY WESTERN WORLD (SINCE 1970)

Outline:

I. From Cold War to Post-Cold War: Toward a New World Order?
    A. The Gorbachev Era
    B. The Gulf War Test

II. Toward a New European Order
    A. Revolution in the Soviet Union
    B. Collapse of the Communist Order in Eastern Europe
    C. The Reunification of Germany
    D. The Disintegration of Yugoslavia
    E. After the Fall
    F. Western Europe: The Winds of Change
    G. From West Germany to Germany
    H. Great Britain: Thatcherism
    I. Uncertainties in France

III. New Directions and New Problems in Western Society
    A. The Women's Movement
    B. Terrorism
    C. The Green Movement

IV. The World of Western Culture
    A. Recent Trends in Art, and Literature
    B. Revival of Religion
    C. Science and Technology
    D. Explosion of Popular Culture

V.   Toward a Global Civilization?
    A.   Global Problems
    B.   Nongovernmental Organizations
    C.   International Cooperation

Key Terms:

1.   Détente   DAY-*TAHNT*

2.   Mikhail Gorbachev   MEEK-*HALE GORE*-BUH-CHOF

3.   *Perestroika*   PAIR-ESS-*TROY*-KAH

4.   *Glasnost*   *GLASS*-NOHST

5.   Andre Sakharov   AHND-*RAY SOCK*-HAHR-OFF

6.   Solidarity   SAHL-UH-*DARE*-UH-TEE

7.   Simone de Beauvoir   SEE-*MOAN* DAY BOOV-*WAH*

8.   Albert Camus   AL-*BEAR* CUH-*MOO*

Questions for Critical Thought:

1.   What directions did the Eastern European nations take once Soviet control ended? Why did they react as they did? Will they change directions again? How and why?

2.   What were the major successes and failures of the Western European democracies after 1970? Was there enough unity among these countries as they sought to create an economic community to succeed?

3.   How did the feminist movement after World War II differ from its pre-war counterparts? Does it now seem at last to have found its true focus?

4.   Explain how modern movements in the arts and philosophy reflect both the uncertainty and the courage to experiment of the recent decades.

5.   Describe the new globalism. How and why did it develop? How does it relate to the technological and social concerns of our age? What might it achieve?

Questions on the Documents:

1. What does Mikhail Gorbachev say made him decide a "restructuring" was necessary? In what sense is it needed everywhere as it is in the Soviet Union?

2. Describe what Vaclav Havel calls the "contaminated moral environment." Who is to blame, and what is the solution? Is this analysis too simple? Why or why not?

3. Explain what Simone de Beauvoir means when she calls woman the "other." Why do men create this stereotype, and why do women tolerate it? Do you agree with her analysis?

4. How does E.F. Schumacher say modern people are using their capital as if it were income? What is his solution? Will it work?